Praise for **AFTER**

"I see the circle of earth/gathered ir [...] poem "First Fruits." And everywhere in this fine collection, Charles Swanson gathers in for his lucky readers the things of this world he refuses to let go. Through poems as heartfelt as they are intelligent, the reader enters with him a distant land—"something akin to Eden"—a land, Swanson reminds us again and again, for which we continue to long. Swanson's voice is as at home with the lyric as with the narrative, as skillful with free verse as with form. Here is a poet who revisits the music and wisdom of the Psalms with a contemporary eye and a masterful hand. *After the Garden* is a triumphant first collection.

– **CATHY SMITH BOWERS**
author of *A Book of Minutes*

Charles Swanson's daily life as nurturer of a family, a small farm, a Baptist congregation and a high school classroom is refracted into poetry in *After the Garden: Selected Responses to the Psalms*. Readers can appreciate these accessible, thought-provoking glances at life, whether or not they triangulate them with the Psalms for additional layers of meaning. They will delight in the sly yet wise juxtapositions of ice-covered trees with osteoporosis, chaos with infinite grace, or the continent with contented space. Boyhood on a small farm provides the recurring center of this poetry, though it ranges to encompass Flannery O'Connor, Johnny Appleseed, Olaudah Equiano and even a stylist proposing a makeover of Jesus. The last line of the last poem, "we go out to feed the present or the future," sums up the nurturing spirit of this poetry and the enticing prospect it affords the reader.

– **GEORGE BROSI**
editor of *Appalachian Heritage*

The comfort of home and farm, mother and grandmother, fills these poems. Among the lasting images is a mother nurturing her son's fantasy by allowing him to drive his toy cars on "porcelain roads" around the eyes of the stove. Another is the loving ritual of a grandmother washing a small boy's dirty feet at day's end. Yet, Charles Swanson does not shy from the pain of labor, the anguish of loss, nor the ravage of time, as evidenced by the poignant description of a grandfather's last harvest of bronzed pumpkins with son and grandson as field hands. Earth colors and life stabilizers anchor the collection, starting with the rich red of tomatoes – and God – and ending with the welcome spring sign of creasy greens – and Mother.

– **GRACE TONEY EDWARDS**
co-editor of *A Handbook to Appalachia*

The poems in Charles Swanson's *After the Garden: Selected Responses to the Psalms* take us back to the true roots of poetry, to its source in prayer, music and the lives of ordinary people who struggle to make sure that the ones who come after them are able to live lives of freedom, hope and faith. In these beautifully-shaped poems about growing up and living in the Virginia Piedmont and Appalachia, Swanson turns ordinary lives into extraordinary prayers. From the first poem to the last, the reader, whether he is a lover of poetry or one who seldom turns to it, will find poems that move and inspire.

– JOHN GUZLOWSKI
author of *Lightning and Ashes*

"This old Bible," Emerson wrote in his Journal (1842), "if you pitch it out the window with a fork, it comes back bounce again," as has happened in TV evangelism. In literature it remains largely missing with, among others, these exceptions: Herman Melville, Walt Whitman, Emily Dickinson, Robert Penn Warren, William Faulkner, Flannery O'Connor and Charles Swanson in *After the Garden*. Here the old shadows in "God-Talk" are present and accounted for, still looming over the land, still disturbing, always teaching.

– ROBERT J. HIGGS
author of *God in the Stadium: Sports and Religion in America*

After the Garden

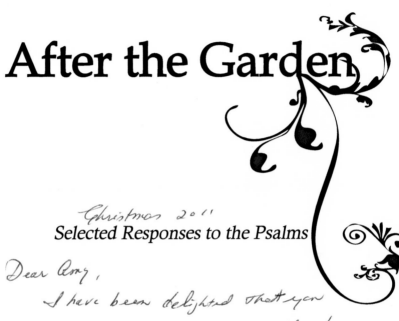

Selected Responses to the Psalms

Christmas 2011

Dear Amy,

I have been delighted that you are in AP Literature with us. You have been a true pleasure, and you are so very gifted. I am an Amy fan!

CHARLES A. SWANSON

Always,

Charles A. Swanson

cswanson@radford.edu

MOTES BOOKS

AFTER THE GARDEN
Selected Responses to the Psalms

Charles A. Swanson

ISBN 978-1-934894-23-1
FICTION

Design
EK LARKEN

Photos
LUCINDA LEE AUSTIN, cover
ANNA LUMMA SWANSON, 91

ACKNOWLEDGEMENTS
The following periodicals have published or have plans to publish the poems cited. Some of these poems appeared in a somewhat different form in the periodicals listed.
ACLA-LINES: "Greening "
ALTAVISTA JOURNAL: "America Realizing Westward: The Poor Man's Dream"
APPALACHIAN HERITAGE: "A Love Song: The Drawing Knife Speaks to Grandfather," "Best Intentions," "First Fruits"
APPALACHIAN JOURNAL: "The Profane and the Holy"
CONFLUENCE: "A Nerveweb of Community—On the Occasion of a Still Exploding," "Palmate," "Osteoporosis and Faith "
THE EMANCIPATOR: "Table Syrup, Cigarettes, and the Blind"
GRAB-A-NICKEL: "Brash Boys, Power Tools, and Welding Helmets," "Fat Dirt," "Where Is My Hero"
NOW & THEN: "Snake Canes for Sale"
PEGASUS: "After the Garden: What Does It Mean, the Killing Fields?"

Louisville, Kentucky

www.MOTESBOOKS.com

Dedication

I saw on a church sign:
"Adam blamed Eve. Eve blamed the snake.
The snake didn't have a leg to stand on."
I send this book out, somewhat like the snake.
After these poems are published, I no longer have a leg to stand on.
I am naked before the world.

God's first garden is still with us, in story, song, sermon and joke.
In one way, my father and mother are my own Adam and Eve,
full of all the mystery of first man and first woman.
I woke in this world to them, and I've always looked to them
for lessons about good and bad, right and wrong.
They taught me of the garden, of joy and of fallen nature.
They taught me to listen for the voice of God,
who still walks in the garden in the cool of the evening.
This book is dedicated to my father, posthumously,
and to my mother, still living.
This book is dedicated to the One
whose cool, insistent voice has always prompted me to write.

– CAS

FROM THE POET

We see in the first few pages of the Bible the picture of Adam and Eve, ashamed of their nakedness. The Psalms show this kind of nakedness, the nakedness of the soul before God. If you find any of these poems troubling, please know that they are not meant to give all the answers. They show the child who is in the monstrous garden of the world—full of thorns, the sweat of the brow, and snakes—as he seeks to find himself, as he seeks to find his God.

– CAS

SELECTIONS

After the Garden

Word Processor

Your name, O Lord, endures forever . . .
Psalm 135:13, RSV

I drop *tomato* and *god*
in the word processor—
hit pulse. The motor whirrs
and the shapes vanish.
As the blades spin, a red
thin chunky substance
splats the glass.

I drop *tomato* on the page

> And Mama Chichi
> garnishes red sauce pizzas
> with yellow bell peppers.
> She watches lovers
> half hidden in patio ferns
> under promenade umbrellas.

I drop tomato on the page

> And a home gardener
> turns up the heat.
> Her stainless steel kettle
> rocks back and forth.
> Ripe tomato ketchup
> dances in sterilized jars.

Tomato

> And pendant globes
> the size of grapefruit
> hang against a southern wall.
> Teenage boys launch
> cherry tomato bombs
> across a school lunchroom.

I drop *god* on the page

> And tomato juice
> is sticky on my hands
> and I cannot wash it off.
> I see a tangled wreath
> with two inch thorns
> and glistening red drops.

I drop god on the page

> And because god
> is on the page someone
> never opened this book.
> Someone else whispers
> god, god, god,
> beside a too-quiet hospital bed.

God

> And a woman packs,
> ready to leave home,
> to live in a third world country:
> God, in fear, in faith,
> to a people who have gods
> because her god tells her to love.

I process words. My friend
gave me a tomato wagon,
a big fat plastic tomato
on tiny wheels, a fanciful bit
of cheap commercial artwork,
a toy. It has a brown yarn string
like a yoke, a tongue, a pull.
It doesn't have an engine,
the wheels don't turn.
It sits mute and motionless
on my study shelf,
but when I look
I find myself in a distant land.

America Realizing Westward: The Poor Man's Dream

Let the nations know that they are but men!
      Psalm 9:20, RSV

The dream of land, not so much a dream
        of continent, but of contented space:
Tidewater, river bottom, or mountain side,
        dense with centuries of oaks, pines,
        or restless as wind-raked prairie,
Some place for common man
        to claim by girdling of trees,
        by running a plowshare in a square,
        turning up that first dark whiff of loam.

The shack he raised would be his home,
        the doorstep, not a proper porch, but his
        to step out to and welcome friends
        or to raise his gun against a foe.
His clothes, the coarsest kind, would stand alone
        from so much salt and sweat,
        too few dashings against wet stones
        in the farm's own watercourse.
But he would raise his head
        from between the handles of the plow
        or above his poor man's walking stick, his hoe,
        to sense this patch of land, his own.

Something akin to Eden for all its thorns,
        its snakes, its hard-won bread.
Something where he, low man that he was
        was rich like Adam, sweetest future of fruit.

Where nations, those that wielded claim or threat,
        were somewhere off behind a mountain range,
        over the ocean's punishing breadth.

He had come this far, needy, hungry, fatherless,
        to beseech the help of God, merciful God,

maker of hurricane, tornado, flood,
designer of thistle, thicket, mud,
keeper of those who have no voice.

He had come
from the midst of his nation's roar,
refugee, to this poor man's shore.

Heirloom Nomenclature

. . . may its fruit be like Lebanon;
and may men blossom forth from the cities
like the grass of the field!
Psalm 72:16, RSV

If seventeen thousand fruit trees
lined up neatly across these hills
I would feel the breath
of Johnny Appleseed's ghost.

Blacktwig, Horse, Cat's Head,
Yellow Sheepnose, Early Harvest,
Winesap, Rusty Coat, Pippin,
Smokehouse, Wolf River, Maiden's Blush.

Copper kettles and drying screens,
peelings like pirouettes
thrown over shoulders, beads
of brown bubbles in gallon jugs.

Widow Norton and Pappy
out on a jamboree,
seasoned wood sparking in the hearth,
the pomology of Monticello.

And every escapee, springing
from undistinguished stock:
a bud bursting, flowering, ripening,
democratic fruiting of the wilderness.

Of Israel, Europe, and Beyond

One generation shall laud thy works to another.
        Psalm 145:4, RSV

Blood says that it has not forgotten
sweep of ridge, lift of fog,
bone a father had begotten,
bone incessant in my bone.

My grandfather's Appalachian barn,
bank barn sunk in hillside earth,
basement stalls cool with darkness
where cattle's eyes get lost in dirt,

is invitation, not grave, but ground
broken off from Scotland,
from heath and moor, cross and mound,
from lichened stones, kirk, and heartland.

I see the fallows, folded hills at morning
where mist is rising. Are these Slovak
fathers, British sires, dissipating?
The fog lisps, *Stop the car and walk.*

Mountain Man, Mountain Myth

We have heard with our ears, O God,
our fathers have told us . . .
Psalm 44:1, RSV

My days are full of pursuit,
    with good walking stick
        or four wheels
    or in later years, mind when body quits.

I have seen him when his head
    whispered white vapors,
        when he called
    by misdirection, mystery in fog.

I have thought about small farms
    impossibly steep
        he once worked
    against gravity, hoe handle a prop.

I have believed he came, too,
    longing to see heights
        or downward
    to valleys like strings, green pearls like new peas.

I have heard smooth-worn stories
    of great-grandfather
        who could dance
    jigs to fiddle tunes, choose such isolation.

Oh, I have heard tell, how quick
    his hand, snatching a
        rattlesnake
    that struck from corn-shocks, stare it eye-to-eye.

How I wish for solitude
    for rattle of leaves

like snake-talk
or high windy moans, mystery, faith-talk.

Come, tell me one more story
about larger men
older days
places that still haunt, talk, give me God-talk.

Infertility

May those who sow in tears
reap with shouts of joy!
Psalm 126:5, RSV

I will plant though the seeds are dry
though the ground is dry,
the field barren.

I will sow in the hills of clay,
though the sky is brass
and shadows fall.

The man in the moon will watch,
question our garden bed,
my husbandry.

With charms and signs, with potions,
I will give my seed,
I will pray.

Day will pass and night, day, night,
moons and tides, cycles,
and we will wait.

And we will sow and sow again,
in the frailness of the flesh,
into the future.

First Fruits

May he remember all your offerings . . .
            Psalm 20:3, RSV

Though this is a love story,
it is not promiscuous.
Quick exits from Cumberland
on Friday evenings
after father's work day
said how much he loved
the southern home
six hours away,
the red clay fields,
the tobacco and sunshine
ripening the summer air,
breathing warmth toward winter.
All this in his look,
in his faraway eyes,
that would fix the highway
like some unthinkable thing
that had to be crossed,
black tar a blankness
for spelling memories
during the dark course
of the evening drive.

Starting early one autumn,
we arrived at the ridge when daylight hung
like scroll work on the old tobacco barn.
Bats were beginning to loop,
but white moths had sun
still in the silk they left on my fingers.

That was the first time I felt
the greeting: something beyond
hugs, kisses, warmth of words.
An invitation
from Granddad to my mother

to see his cucumber patch
upslope from the barn.

Above the old tobacco beds
where young plants had been drawn
to set the now maturing fields.

She didn't have a sack,
The car was empty
of bucket, poke, and bag,
nothing to gather cucumbers
but the old tin can smelling
of rust and emergency stops.
It represented haste,
not the destination.
It would not do.

So Mama took herself,
dressed as she was,
while Granddad guided her
past decaying logs
that once elevated cloth,
cloth mesh like milkweed fluff
over spring seedlings the size of ticks,
but now lay like logs of crocodiles
waiting in waist-high weeds,
late summer's neglected jungle.

Not quite sure,
about the attraction
of a rocky hillside,
of weeds and waste,
I watched them.
Watched with shadows
coming down.
Granddad stooped and handed
green sticks to Mama
who bunched her skirt,

gathered its pleats
in one schooled hand,
and filled the cloth with fruit.

They stumbled back to the car,
tripping in morning glory vines,
overgrown fescue, lespedeza,
Mama with her skirt, the circle of the earth,
gathered to make a poke.
Cucumbers tumbled free
when she released the hem.
We stacked them, plantbed logs
in the floorboard of the Ford.
Mama fussed about the marks
where the fresh-plucked stems
had bled against the cloth.

Washings never released
the stains of cucumbers,
nor miles the sight
of earth's long jewels
brought to the car in a cotton dress,
nor years the smile
on Granddad's face.

With twilight
we drifted down the ridge side,
under fireflies and starfields
to the home house by the creek.
Night sang, frogs sang,
as we lugged love's labor,
green cucumbers,
to the kitchen table.

Fields and houses, kitchen tables,
change,
weeds grow beyond bounds,

she is older than he,
and he is gone.
But we talk
of her father-in-law, my grandfather.
Reared back beside her kitchen table,
sipping coffee,
I see his love of growing things,
I hear her honor his life,
I see why I grapple with weeds
through the sweat of summer,
I see the circle of the earth
gathered in a cotton dress.

A Love Song:
The Drawing Knife Speaks to Grandfather

. . . thou givest them drink
from the river of thy delights.
Psalm 36:8, RSV

I bite
when your hands are too rough,
and your hands are rough
from hoe handle and axe haft,
from hefting sawmill boards and fieldstones.

I handle,
when you touch me smoothly,
with the long stroke, the gentle pull,
by curling away golden shavings,
by inviting you with spicy smells of wood.

I fashion
your mind's eye, your heart's hope,
in the hushed world of morning,
by the light of the workshop doorway,
sun falling on your brown arms, my bright blade.

We wed
moments to hours, perspiration to vision,
a chair slat, a table leg, a cradle—
warmth of a newborn from well-aged stock,
wood, and man, and tool.

Doing the Hundreds

For Bessie Eva Ramsey who died at the age of 106

Faithfulness will spring up from the ground . . .
and our land will yield its increase.
Psalm 85:11,12, RSV

Grandma's slow swing through life, a field,
broad, wide, sun-sweet
clover. Such hay
hundreds of days

could not cut. Down her life came, blade
by blade. Such weight—
what lay before
acted to shore,

like braces, what was falling. Scythe sweep
so slow, to teach
us, watching, faith—
the strength of days.

Old Time Foot Washing

He raises the poor from the dust . . .
Psalm 113:7, RSV

We rough little boy cousins
had all day played Swamp Fox,
a game we invented
and named after Francis Marion.
We also dreamed of the War general
Mosby, the Gray Ghost of the Confederacy,
who melted into the hills of Virginia,
playing hide and seek with Union troops.
Curtis and I were always Billy Yank,
despite our protests. All day
over Southside piedmont hills
we looked for some distant shirt-tail
of Tommy and Bob, the Rebs.
I can see them yet, standing in a sloping pasture,
the sun catching the distant grins,
the wave of arms in defiance,
before they disappear in thicket.
Curtis and I run to the spot, panting,
both slower, heftier, younger.
We look for tracks, pretend to be sharp-eyed
Union Scouts, keen to hoofprints
(a good steed paws the earth as he rears)
but can find no trace of bare feet
in the broom-straw pasture.
After our mock search, sweating bullets,
we take off, head in the direction
we saw them go fifteen minutes earlier.
All day, up to the old tobacco barn on the ridge,
down along rushing Turkeycock,
holing up to breathe under the creek bridge
where the water swirls,
we spend the day in glimpses, we spend the day
chasing our beloved enemies.

All of that, and yet when shadows fall,
and bedtime is pushed upon us,
I am not ready. Mama has to scold.
I let Grandma
wash my dirt-stained red clay feet.
Grandma makes ritual:
the wood stove stoked, the water warming
in the stainless steel,
the straightback chairs pulled to face each other.
She spreads her aproned lap to hold
both pan and outstretched foot.
It disappears in the foam of suds.
She scrubs, cleans with the rag between toes,
across the callused heel. Like a good
little boy I squirm, and yet
I can stand it.
It comes back as the sweetest moment
in the long sweet days.
Rosy warmth radiates from toe tip
to knee joint. The feet of clay
disappear
under Grandma's ministrations.

The Farmwife Grades

Readying Tobacco for Market, Prince George, Virginia, 1960s

I am reckoned among those who go down to the Pit . . . .
Are thy wonders known in the darkness,
or thy saving help in the land of forgetfulness?
Psalm 88:4,12, RSV

From late August to November I live
like a mole except for the naked light
bulb over my head and the tiny window
with two panes in the corner near the joist.
Or maybe a bear, except I don't sleep,
spending every day huddled in the pit

and into the night, too, grading. The pit's
a lonesome place, not where I'd choose to live,
and when I go to the house to sleep
I grade tobacco leaves in my dreams: a light
lemon here, brown there, leaves piled to the joist,
and not even a bird at the window

to remind me of outdoors. The window
ought to be right in front, so the dark pit
would seem a picture show. I would take joy
in looking out, seeing something alive.
Swimming on the pond. Ducks or geese lighting.
Fish breaking in circles. The autumn sleep

that sheets the pond in ice. Instead, I sleep
grading and grade sleeping. The dim window
trades places with the dull bulb, light for light,
leaf for leaf, day for night, fall for this pit.
I'd like to be kicking fall leaves, how live
they seem, soaked in evening rains. But this joist

shuts me in. Flying clouds for a low joist
is not worth the money. It is a sleep

like death, to pile the crop around you, live
like a spider, where even one window
hurts, because it reminds you of the pit,
that you've been assigned to hide from the light.

I will teach my boys to walk in the light
even when they join me under this joist,
in this damp concrete hole, this rank earth pit.
Their talk will spark my day, rouse me from sleep,
take me down hallways of school—a window
into their world—and I will laugh at their lives.

Their light limbs dance, even sitting. They'll sleep
sweetly, quilts for a joist, dreams for windows,
and the pit will speak family—love and life.

Osteoporosis and Faith

For my life is spent with sorrow,
and my years with sighing;
my strength fails because of my misery,
and my bones waste away.
Psalm 31:10, RSV

The trees say, *This* is tired.
Ice coats
their shoulders, bends their backs,
makes the humps of their spines
more pronounced. They have been all day
at looking to their feet
where a fractured kaleidoscope
litters the ground,
throws back glimpses of blue and white
in shards.
They are dazed, overburdened.
Ice crinkles from their brittleness,
tinkling down,
and sometimes limbs crash, too,
prefatory of a greater fall.

So the women, my aunts,
my mother,
as the sun moves their limbs
toward winter.
A whiteness crowns them, weight
of days, their shoulders
creak toward their chests. Flesh
sheens and wanes; bones brittle,
break under precipitated stress.
They seem only fit
for looking down:
worry, their burdens, others;
inexplicable gravity
stoops them.
Life seems shattered at their feet.

But they do not forget,
these fragile women.
The brilliant heaps of brokenness
still reflect the sky.

My Mother and I Celebrate My Birthday at Stanleytown Nursing Home

For he knows our frame;
he remembers that we are dust.
Psalm 103:14, RSV

A curious midpoint, age fifty-two,
and leaves hanging still on Turkeycock,
the mountain that dominates my view.
My parents, uncle and aunt, took buckets
and picked huckleberries from the banks
along the fire road on the mountain's ridge,
summers and summers ago. And now my aunt,
a small shrub struck by a freeze, withers.
As Mom and I drive to Stanleytown, I muse.
Did the leaves hang late the fall I was born?
I think of all the birthday cards she sent,
never missing my day. Her eyelids droop
with the white-blue of frost, of age and morphine.
We call her name, but can't tell if she wakes or sleeps.

A Higher Power

For the King trusts in the Lord . . . .
        Psalm 21:7, RSV

I need someone infallible.
When I was four, I didn't know the word,
but someone who could manage trouble,

someone who had skirts, when my heart was full
where I could hide my face when eyesight blurred.
I needed someone infallible.

Wisdom became more inscrutable
as I saw mother's mistakes, as I heard
of someone who could manage trouble

by finding it. A foundation crumbled
somewhere. Who could pronounce that final word?
I needed someone infallible.

I love her all the more. I tremble
as I become the parent, she the child.
But someone who can manage trouble

I need, and need the more. Rubble
is the end of flesh. How does flesh become the Word?
I need someone infallible.
I need someone who can manage trouble.

After the Garden:
What Does It Mean, the Killing Fields?

For I know my transgressions,
and my sin is ever before me.
Psalm 51:3, RSV

Now this is the truth:
If there is sin, sin beyond
the thorns and the sweat of the brow, then
I have eaten.

We ran through the swamp woodlands,
blasting hummocks of litter like puffballs,
the bunny zagging through patches of light,
my mother with the twenty gauge,
I with a mouthful of marbles,
hard questions that choked me.
She shot a log from under his leap—
mossy wood showering green fireworks,
the somersaulting figure
an acrobat landing on his feet.
He slipped the skin of earth,
in the hollow trunk of a tree.
Putting aside the gun,
she reached a long arm up to armpit
into the mystery of darkness
to grasp his warm hind foot,
pads like buttercups, smooth as wax.
He came out lank, sinews stretched,
long last the tender twitching ears.
We sank onto the mossy log
damaged by her errant shot
and she laid the rabbit along her lap.
Her left hand gripped his feet,
and with her right she swaddled his head
in caress or stranglehold.
The rabbit made a squeaking noise
and I choked out

one hard marble. "Mama,
what will you do?"
A practiced hand made the wrenching sound.

These are the killing fields.
Out of the milk of human kindness
I have been fed.

Strange Country

By the waters of Babylon,
there we sat down and wept
when we remembered Zion.
Psalm 137:1, RSV

Behind the cold stove,
the dark oil circulator,
I made Babylon.

I don't remember
why I pitied myself so,
such a childish act.

I wanted kindness,
thought by crying my mother
would cradle me.

I deserved scolding,
scolding that sent me upstairs
to sob in the night.

Accountable at
six, but still, still, Babylon
sometimes captures me,

darkness washed with strings
of minor music, foreign
waters even yet.

Excesses

It is he who remembered us in our low estate,
for his steadfast love endures forever.
Psalm 136:23, RSV

With my mother's permission
        we knocked out a quarter-panel
        in my bedroom door, a narrow route
        like a tunnel through the wall
        of the county jail. A melodrama,
the prison bars were the iron rails
        of the old baby bed in the room's corner,
        sides let down to make a dark dungeon.
        We embellished a handbill—
        The Gunslinger's Escape.

Years earlier, six hours from cousins,
        I loaded my dumptruck
        with caterpillar corpses,
        drove them to my mother's feet,
        and dissected for their green blood.
That same pockmarked backyard
        made a country for my cars and trucks.
        I visited for hours,
        motoring up to hillocks of grass,
        saying hello to relatives.

The galvanized milkbox by the back door
        housed the dreamland of toys
        when I came inside. The milkman,
        the good guy dressed all in white,
        relinquished the day's milk to the steps.
On inclement days in western Maryland,
        I brought my cars inside, and Mama
        let me pull up to the kitchen stove
        drive the porcelain roads of the range,
        stopping at each electric eye to say Howdy.

Acknowledgements to the dreaming life,
     to the small mind questing in the world,
     all these excesses, where Mama
     let the little boy fantasize
     toward the man within me—

yet, in the sanctuary when the cup and bread
     were passed, when I wanted communion,
     and light fractured through the stained glass
     hands of Jesus, she would whisper,
     not yet; you are not yet saved.

Brash Boys, Power Tools, and Welding Helmets

Every one utters lies to his neighbor;
with flattering lips and a double heart they speak . . .
The promises of the Lord are promises that are pure . . .
Psalm 12:2,6, RSV

Knowing the aggressive eighth grade boy—
headlong leaps off scaffoldings,
tools launched across the shop like footballs,
chair legs turned into toothpicks,
demolition over construction
because he delights in smashing things—
Mr. Glass gave his speeches repeatedly.
In the relative safety of the Ag classroom,
he told of boys losing fingers to blades
(blood like a mountain spring gushing),
of nails shot into flesh like harpoons
from errant hammer swings,
of eyes blinded by arcs like the sun,
told and retold in matter-of-fact
death-dealing precision.

Perhaps the mind is not welded
(riveted, nailed, pegged, glued, or circuited)
to the body of an eighth grade boy.
I certainly never determined
what was truth and what hyperbole.
Boys I never understood anyway
rushed into shop like runaway stock
breaking through rusted boundaries.
Brash as the noonday light,
they poured toward power tools,
the voice of Mr. Glass dim and fragile.
And I, familiar as I was with whirring
mowers, chain saws, combines, tractors,
looked at each tool like an enemy
rattling a preordained warning.

The flashings of caution sizzled
like the light patterns fracturing
from the doorways of welding booths.
But for many boys, what flashed were smiles
under goggles, over lathes or radial saws,
to other boys at their elbows,
boasts above the whines and screams,
surely the bragging of a battlefield.
Alone, with a rectangle of iron,
I fitted the heavy helmet over my eyes,
trying to strike a spark, light a rod.
The green glow of the flowing metal
held an eerie beauty, dream-like, unearthly.
There was more to see than my eyes could see,
for I saw through a glass darkly.

Where Is My Hero

They surrounded me like bees,
they blazed like a fire of thorns . . .
Psalm 118:12, RSV

If I knew the large hearts of heroes
I would not see you in a dreamscape.

I am there, the sun and shade blending,
cool for an early summer evening
on the Danville Community College lawn,
parents celebrating with their teenagers
governor's school achievements.
The talk is too bright—the uncertain
laughter like the lightfall
on the uneven tree-draped yard.

So I see you running
and I hear the screams—
I think on a movie screen.
They can do these tricks
with sound and time—freeze frame
and slow-motion. My darkened seat
at the patio table is wide angle.
I struggle to my feet. How
can I move so slowly?
The action on a repeating
loop, you run straight
through dumbfounded
freeze-framed people
right to the screaming girl—
your classmate, lift her,
carry her up the lawn.
She is still in panic. I am saying
What's happening?
What's wrong? I learn
she has stumbled
into a nest of yellow-jackets.

An innocuous evening
suddenly turns bizarre,
danger in the swirl
of pleasantries,
and who can respond?

Every time I see you running
every time I hear her terror
I wonder, *Why can't I
get up from my seat?*

The Devil's Playground

Aha, Aha!
        Psalm 40:15, RSV

I remember pines. To the left
of his shoulder, the oblique sun
deepening the black boles,
trunks towering over hardpacked dirt.

I remember his chambray shirt,
a crosshatch; my own shirt
crushed against my damp back,
grass clumps gritting through fabric.

I remember what I don't remember,
his actual face, his name.
I remember happy, flinty eyes,
teeth full of triumph.

I remember how undogged I lay,
how unferret my spirit,
his knees knuckled in my gut,
how dumb animal, docile,

how I should have squirmed, hissed,
hunched for his bowels.
I remember a lamb at slaughter.
I should have fought harder. Harder!

Why do I remember something
so trivial?—So visceral!
Why does the urge to fight gorge me
when I want to be humble?

Sweet Pea

He keeps all his bones;
        not one of them is broken.
            Psalm 34:20, RSV

She says the bundle floated through the air.
She saw the car, the arm that flicked the child.
The baby drifted into safety there

Between the four lane road. His halo hair
Shone in the morning sun. Oh, she was wild,
she says. The bundle floated through the air,

through waters, wrapped in bulrushes, prayers.
They sailed Moses in the fierceness of the Nile.
The baby drifted into safety there,

And Pharaoh's daughter claimed him. All ask where,
where is the mother? The witness is wild
who says the bundle floated through the air.

They find the reason for her wild despair.
She is the mother. How hope, a tiny child,
a baby, drifted into safety here

in emergency, and so many care
about this child, despite the mother's guile.
She says the bundle floated through the air.
The baby drifted into safety here.

To Pray, To Do

Here is where
reflection turns to prayer.
Give me courage and
unstopper me.

Prayer for an Unclosing

In the day of my trouble I seek the Lord;
in the night my hand is stretched out . . .
Psalm 77:2, RSV

A blown Carolina rose hides no pistil.
Its sexual organs lie revealed,
yellow stamens couched on pink sheets,
naked and fingered by a mild breeze.
But the hand I reach forth is not that open,
a fist, clutched like the hybrid tea, fold on fold.
Dew may bead its outside, hard tears,
and fingers must be pried, petal by petal,
to get at last to what is hidden, shame, or grief,
or sin. And yet the arm extends the hand.

To God. And God replies, stretching
a clutch of lightning bolts, thunder, downpour,
wind, to rip roofs from rafters, siding
from skeletal studs, leaves in a maelstrom
all over the park. In the morning, shattered roses
litter the garden, make a riot of boxwood walkways—
chaos, infinite grace, to blow open the heart.

Living with Danger

1.
Craft for Distress

He will cover you with his pinions,
and under his wings you will find refuge . . .
Psalm 91:4, RSV

A seed rooster: each vocalization of corn,
syllable of butterbean, echo of lentil or split pea,
lacquered, tuned, so that even in a dark room
the artwork sings. The seeds argue dialectic,
antiphonal response, to a categorical
list of woes: arthritis, neuralgia, cancer.

I visit your dark home where artwork
is the only hint of happiness.
No one could have predicted
the accident that took your son. But I see
your hands selecting seeds, rubbing pregnant disks
between thumbs, rolling round simples
in your palm to feel smooth skins.
I see your eyes, twins to brown persimmon orbs
glow like amber mirrors at each tortoise back
of speckled bean, each strong gray stripe
of sunflower seed. I see you take life,
encased though it is in horny shells,
and shape a high stepping, fierce-eyed bird,
a rooster to echo a challenge
down your long lonely years.

2.
Shoeless

On their hands they will bear you up
lest you dash your foot against a stone.
Psalm 91:12, RSV

A farmboy's feet are tough. Southern fields cook
on summer days. The sun glints off mica.
The woods hide holly leaves, barbs like pinchers
on a crawdad. Everywhere I look,
or don't look, in hayfields and row crops,
nettles hide. The thorns on berry briars
break off, deep in the skin. But these are minor.
Pitchforks, rusty nails, pruning hooks
lie poised like adders. Amazing how they strike
as if taught by a malevolent power.
I once left a sewing needle unstuck.
It jumped off the table for my brother's foot
And bit through flesh, fanged against bone. Hours
it took of probing to get to the root of the bite.

Leaf-Fall

When his breath departs he returns to his earth . . .
          Psalm 146:4, RSV

Out of earshot, Dad urges me to the field,
Grandpa's last harvest. The corn didn't make,
but pumpkins did. He knows this is vacation—
Grandpa's, where he lets me run free. He pleads,
says I might not have him long. One brown leaf
ripples on my teenage mind. I lay
fat bronze pumpkins in the wagon bed,
hear Dad and Grandpa's murmur in the field.
When Grandpa enters the Chatham men's room,
we are back home. Graffiti and piss stains.
White hair and bib overalls on concrete.
Now Dad's steps slow, his back stiffens.
I look for fields of pumpkins as I drive
and my head fills up with the brownness of leaves.

The Profane and the Holy
(Hog killing on the day before Thanksgiving)

He who has clean hands and a pure heart . . .
    Psalm 24:4, RSV

He flinches as blood
splatters on his neck and arms.
The stuck hog still jerks.

He grasps the tire chains,
works his side of the black tub,
grabs handfuls of hair.

The body comes clean.
Water washes flesh rosy.
Mud, scurf, scald away.

His wet coveralls
seem thin in late autumn gusts,
freeze along the cuffs.

His heavy boots squish.
Hog pen mud clumps the leather,
stiffens the laces.

He looks at his hands:
black seams vein his puckered palms,
grime lines his fingers,

deep dirt that darkens
tomorrow. How will he come
clean for Thanksgiving?

Poem at Freezing

. . . thou hast made him little less than God,
and dost crown him with glory and honor.
Psalm 8:5

even unpracticed,
the child's hand,
guiding the snips of scissors
into the five-time folded sheet,
evokes a starry snowflake—
something sparkles like snowflakes
in her eyes.

how raindrops freeze,
making not one
automaton shape—
die-stamped, tooled, and serialized,
cranked out in assembly line,
but fingerprints, whorls,
passports to faraway,
as different as noses, thumbs, toes.
how snow lace
fluffs like a winter white sale,
or builds crenellated barricades
on breastwork of forest-fort,
pings like gray steelies
on galvanized tin,
ices like hair gel—
slick on black tar surfaces.

the housewife picks up the thread,
shaping snow-white crochet
chain by chain. pineapples,
spiderwebs, granny squares,
pansies, whirl
in and out of snowflakes,
land on every surface,
dinner table, arm chair,

dresser top.
light shines from lamps
on expanses of white,
reflects from windowpanes
that crochet drapes.
in winter, when day breaks
to night snow, and snow questions
riddle the window glass,
an answer rimes from inside,
made by a similar hand at play.
a greater and lesser creator
have touched palm to palm,
have pressed five-fingered
star to five-fingered star
against the glass, enchanting
all away but the invisible barrier
between two worlds.

Palmate

Make a joyful noise unto the Lord, all the earth . . .
            Psalm 98:4, RSV

Running, I stopped to pick a sycamore leaf
Because I thought of love. Five miles to run,
I bent its old and leathery skin, a sheaf
Of oil-rich parchment, dyed by rain and sun,
The particular temperament of the tree, and all
That signifies adversity, I bent five
Leaf fingers closed, its palm against my palm,
And ran. I had not expected such a live
Response. Leaves are supposed to feel dry—
Nothing like flesh. My hand clenched to keep
The leaf from flying, I ran, sweated, wrote,
Not with a pen on leaf, as poets dream,
But vein to vein, its shape touching my life
Lines, whispering its own love note.

From a Parched Land

O, for rain in abundance, O God . . .
        Psalm 68:9, RSV

I haven't traveled, haven't seen dry Sinai,
the land that flowers rocks more readily than vines.
I haven't seen Elijah's drought or strained to spy
a cloud, hand-small, over the Mediterranean
or run with robe's ends tucked about my loins
ahead of pounding rain. The Israelites know dry,
know the stagnant cistern and the goat's flat teats,
know the fruitless search of the bee on desert heights.
The cow goes dry and the honeycomb hardens
out my own back door. I walk through twisted corn,
in cracking fields where clover's shrunk to its roots.
I begin to smell pickled, like a man in brine.
I turn my nose at my own sour sweetness.
The sky is dead, and sweat runs down to my boots.

Headwaters

If I take the wings of morning
and dwell in the uttermost parts of the sea,
even there thy hand shall lead me . . .
Psalm 139:9-10, RSV

I want to know where the small streams go,
at the head of watersheds, the tiny
creeks gurgling through buttercup weed
and orchard grass, over sparkling
smooth-ground waterwashed stones.

The spirit of God is moving

I study maps, green topography,
wavering lines of elevation.
Over boundaries, destinations,
I sigh, over swift capillaries,
waterways in God's wild bloodstream.

over the face of the waters.

My brain is a map of valleys,
intricate as the Appalachians.
I write fantasies in my mind
just so I can chart water courses,
just so I can make a way to the sea.

The spirit of God is moving
over the face of the waters.

A Way of Life

They have neither knowledge nor understanding . . .
Psalm 82:5, RSV

Now, it was a mighty hot time
a dry, scalding July,
and Millard knew I had moonshine,
so we took a little ride

down to the lake, loaded the car
from some jars I had stored.
I guess I had me five, six cases
of white half gallon liquor.

Well, we went to drink, so we drank,
sitting with the doors open
when Millard, stretching, hit the gear shift,
and the car started rolling.

It jumped, just like it had a mind,
down across the steep woods
and flung itself in a bunch of bushes.
We found we were tight shut-up,

couldn't budge a door. So we drank.
That was what we'd come for.
We drank from Wednesday to Saturday.
We had quite a little store.

It was hot like you wouldn't believe,
I think it was the heat,
in a hollow in the thicket's shade
with the dry droning of bees.

Rennie found us on that Saturday,
saw the tail of the car below.
They knew we were missing and he had
some idea where to look.

They drove me to Roanoke Memorial,
kept me several days.
They didn't take Millard with me
for he had long gone away.

A Nerveweb of Community
— On the Occasion of a Still Exploding

Surely the wrath of men shall praise thee;
the residue of wrath thou wilt gird upon thee.
Psalm 76:10, RSV

Luther Riddle, at the country store:
I watched it from my own front porch. I sat in the evening,
unlacing my shoes, the sweat drying on my back. Bugs was
popping the window screens. Maybe, in the shadows, the boys
didn't see me as they pulled the truck down the old red washout.
One of them was holding it by the coil. I thought he ought to have
it by the retort. They bumped on down the pig path out of sight,
and didn't know I saw, or didn't care. It may be back in the hollow,
but it ain't hidden.

Royall Cousins, at the firehouse:
I seen so many botched jobs. Sometimes they push it too hard. Or
they conceal it in a barn and don't even use the flue holes and the
stove pipes that are right there. Let the heat just build and build.
Don't know how they stand so close to the flames, pushing locust
wood into the stove, stoking the fire beyond reason. Alcohol burns,
you know. Goes up like tarnation. You'll lose your eyebrows and a
whole lot more if you don't step lively.

Clydene Napier, down the road a bit:
I saw the world ending right before my eyes. The revival preacher
had told the second coming hot and heavy. He stomped, flung his
arms around, crooned to us, singsong, about the intense burning,
how fire was being prepared for the unrepentant, how we would be
left behind in backyard gardens, at our sewing machines, at kitchen
sinks with our hands plunged wrist deep in sudsy water.

Then I drove home in the stillness, black as the underside of a bed.
Not a star shining anywhere. My headlights cutting the dark, and
the road empty. That's when the sky lit up—orange, red, rosy-pink.
All so sudden, so glorious. The horizon was a halo. Daylight had
descended, and I knew it was the Lord. I said, right there in the car,

"Jesus, I'm ready." But he didn't come for me.

I drove on to the house under that eerie sky. Nobody was to
home. Russell was nowhere to be seen, and I said, "Lord, you've
taken him and left me." I walked from room to room, touching
keepsakes I'd bought at Pigeon Forge, Myrtle Beach, like that was
all I was left with, some thimbles, vinegar cruets, ceramic cats. I
circled through the house, stopping at the kitchen window, thought
about the prophecy of sudsy dishwater, looked out at the radiant
sky glimmering over the tree tops.

When Russell came home, he found me in the bottom of his closet
where I'd fallen asleep, curled up in the middle of his shoes, found
me holding onto one of his old work shirts. I remember touching
it, thinking I'd never see him again, smelling for his sweat that I'd
tried so hard to wash out and now wanted back.

Jesus and His Stylist

Yea, dogs are round about me;
a company of evildoers encircle me;
they have pierced my hands and feet—
Psalm 22:16, RSV

Now, first I must cut your hair.
You look like a Hippie:
Retrofitted, fortunately minus the love beads.
You've got that unbleached robe thing going—
and those walked-over sandals!
Your face is too passive,
and that gaunt, hollowness about your cheeks,
somehow—you know—makes you intellectual, and
that spells *out-of-touch*.
But, your eyes, with that heavy-lidded drooping stare,
there are fires . . . We've just got to make them pop.
I can see passion—
but you also look—
what's the right word? Unambitious?

Now, that's better. That military style cut
fits your head—just *sings* alertness,
and that gray microfiber suit
drapes just right. Why, I'm not sure, but
with the short hair, you don't look emaciated.
You look lean and muscled,
tigerish.
And your eyes.
Where did those skewers come from?
They're nails, man, nails.
What acuity!

With that signature look,
I can see you moving in the twenty-first century.
You'll rise up through skyscrapers,
through levels of steel and glass,
the city beneath your feet,
briefcase and Rolex saying class, class, class.

And confidence, man, confidence!
You'll move past the office carrels
and they'll turn their heads.
They'll surprise themselves because they'll look around,
convicted by your *puissance*.
They won't expect such authority.
You see how I'm your perfect publicist?
We'll plan the most ambitious take-over.
We'll have the whole world talking.
What more could you want?

Deliveries

May our sons . . . be like plants . . .
our daughters like corner pillars . . . .
May our cattle be heavy with young . . .
Psalm 144:12,14, RSV

1.

I went to the hospital to see her, knowing this
miscarriage was not her first.

I was green, not accustomed to hospital visits,
not accustomed to loss,
other than miscarriages I'd seen
as a boy on the farm.

She was nothing like the cat
screaming and dragging
across the hayloft's rough boards,
trying to dislodge the stuck shut-eyed kitten.
I had run. How could I help a screeching
clawing cat?

She lay as empty, as full, as I had seen. Pale,
her gown the lightest washed out color,
her face brimming in her eyes.
I spoke softly.
At just one or two words
her cheeks glistened.

I remember the elevator
as I descended,
the feeling of the bottom
dropping out.

A prayer was safety
for I could close my eyes.
I prayed for her
and I prayed for me.

2.

I waited at the church.
Deacon Henry Lee, a good old boy, was running late.

He came in fifteen minutes,
break-neck, tumbling out of his truck.
His apology and petition
mingled in a rush of words.

He said I was a farm boy,
I could help, couldn't I?
His neighbor's cow was struggling to give birth.
We could make that stop our first visit.

I smiled to myself thinking of barnyards,
manure, a slick calf half-born,
afterbirth. Yes, I knew farms.
And we would make more visits?

But I went. Henry Lee
introduced me, his new preacher,
as we walked to the stable.
I took off my shirt.

The young cow stood still,
(and I thank the Lord for that).
The narrowness of the birth canal,
the wrenching, rotating hunt for nose and feet,
the pulling until our joints cracked,
and the calf came. Soft blue hoof,
clot filled nose, inch by inch,
until shoulders, flank,
tail slid out. It tottered and wheezed,
snuffed a strangled breath,
opened eyes with a wet look
on a bright new world.

We did make more stops.
After I kicked my shoes through the grass,
washed up in the neighbor's sink,
lathered fingers, arms, chest, stomach,
I put my shirt back on,
got in Henry Lee's truck,
and we continued our delivery,
the gospel's glorious good news.

A New Litany for Response

Minister: "Our sanctuaries are destroyed, O Lord."
People: "O Lord, grant us sanctuary."

Do not deliver the soul of thy dove to the wild beasts . . .
Psalm 74:19, RSV

The white shirt smudged with soot,
soot black as his black pants, black tie,
and puffs of charcoal where his foot

treads scorched timbers. He comes by
the yellow tape, dressed for church,
with black face, black as the smashed sky.

He comes out of his pile of church,
where he should not be this morning, past crew
in fall-out gear, who have responded, lurched

like men on a mission, crazed saviors, through
traffic, curves. Too late. Heads bowed, they let
him in the ruins, depressed themselves. And who

could stop the smoky eyes of this prophet?
He looks like wilderness. Gray ash is flaked
onto his pomaded hair, and his knotted

hands ball and pull. He makes
his way past a sign, red-splayed and crooked,
to his flock. Some are writhing like snakes.

All are speechless. Stunned. They look
to him, their preacher, to make sense
out of destruction. He has his book

in his vest pocket. Its white unstained
leather smudges in his hands
as he fumbles for a Psalm. He hides pain

behind calm words. "In the land
they have burned the synagogues of God.
Arise, O God, stretch out your hand,

plead your cause." The sign is plywood,
crudely lettered. *Death To All Blacks*
is splashed in a red that looks like blood.

He kicks the whiskey bottle back
into a scorched bush. Everyone is silent
as he bows his head, bends his back,

and kneels. The smoke-rimmed sun glints
off glass, casts the shadow of the black cross
over them. The old man prays, "Repent,
all you who fear the Lord. Repent."

Ashes to Ashes, Dust to Dust

For all our days pass away under thy wrath,
our years come to an end like a sigh.
Psalm 90:9, RSV

I sweep the ash toward an uneven edge
of dustpan. The hardwood floor becomes a page

where bits of burnt wood, charcoal, soot
are swept over and over, then mashed underfoot

to form a child's first scrawled attempt
to write an alphabet, or Joseph's blasted dream-grain

of ears and ears of smut. How quickly labor burns,
smoke up the flue, ashes in the stove, turned

from sweat and something solid into heat,
a few warm moments followed by ashes and black feet.

The Valley of the Shadow

1.
Me and My Shadow

Surely man goes about as a shadow!
       Psalm 39:6, RSV

A shadow,
       upslope,
              bent in a most unnatural place
       for my corporeal flesh—
              diagonally
       hip to shoulder
              like a sash—
       intangible foldup
              against a cliff.
       And long legs laid,
              flush to land
       in shadow shape,
              like part of me
       has been, thus early,
              laid to rest.

And if this vision
       shudders the heart, I have,
              for now, to think
       that it will pass,
              the day will end,
       the sun go down.

A deeper darkness will descend.

2.
Decay

For I am thy passing guest, a sojourner,
like all my fathers.
                    Psalm 39:12, RSV

Even inside the truck, one morning I
Could feel the hush that mists the drowsy land.

Mists I say, for mists will smother sound.
And sun was tentative as well, but hints,

Despite my facing east. It hid itself
Behind the age-old ridge. And gray-green moss

Was crumbling asphalt shingles into dust,
Edge by edge, upon the faint gray house

Beside the road. I thought, *This is decay,*
But beautiful, and marveled at myself.

I stepped into a cramped old chicken house,
One time, that leaned toward oblivion. Vines

Wreathed it, wrenched it earthward, where the floor
Was more like wormwork or rich soil than wood.

I need this, I thought. It smelled of dirt, of age,
Of something subtle, wood notes, my cologne,

Born in firepits or working yeast. And green
Smells wound their way through cracks and claimed it

And me. And Grandma, who was seamed and soft
And falling toward decay, sunken, slackmouthed,

Because she chewed, was like an angel. Rays
Of childhood light suffuse her in my dreams.

She is effusive as mist, though laid to rest.
But a morning's moment on my way to work.

Southern Cemeteries

*Truly no man can ransom himself,
or give to God the price of his life . . .*
Psalm 49:7, RSV

In Flannery O'Connor's Christ-haunted landscape
the Holy Ghost stretches his shadow
over every corner of the South.
His spirit filters, transfigures,
even intense August days,
breathing a heat chill into afternoons.

How many uncles, grandfathers, have tended
graveyard plots where ground sinks
before markers and headstones lean.
Those same grandfathers may not have darkened
the pews of Sunday's sanctuaries,
but they have sanctuaried the dead.

My elderly next-door neighbor, a cripple,
fought blackberry and poison ivy
down the hill below my house.
He marked the resting place of slaves
with iron moldboards from old plows
though he didn't know a name.

A certain diligence we call respect
that fills the grizzled forms of ones
who hallow every planting
on the farm—they seem to droop
limbs like heat-hazed cedars
that lay their shadows on the grass.

Pantry

Thou hast kept count of my tossings;
put thou my tears in thy bottle!
Are they not in thy book?
Psalm 56:8, RSV

Jar on jar, saved, shelved.
Light through the western window
reflects, splinters, sleeps.

Tears, tears, tears, to make
a bottle. Were they eyedropped
from wet cheeks to glass?

Tweezed? Does God tweeze tears?
Do feather-fingered chopsticks
lift them one by one?

And why count my tears?
They are not incense, perfume,
to dash beneath God's ears.

Stale, before they fell,
desolate drops, bitter, undone,
not condensed faith, hope.

Why would God save tears?
Unless to brush heart, head, cheek,
brush and say, *I know.*

I have bottled them,
colorless, like wind, spirit,
breath. Full, not empty.

Fat Dirt

Thy crownest the year with thy bounty;
the tracks of thy chariot drip with fatness.
Psalm 65:11, RSV

I boil the cracklings down, huddled
in my coat, on an upended stick
of firewood. The heat has drawn

a magic circle against the frost.
The morning stretches, and the sprites
that dance in whitened grass

disappear. The fire sizzles, spits,
as globes of oil bubble, pop,
and arc out of the blackened pot.

The ground grows rich about my feet.
I cook away all morning, tending
the melting fat with my paddle,

hand-hewn, drawn from hickory wood.
It is slicked with the golden oil,
lustrous grain of dark heart's core,

of light-hued, fine-tongued edge.
It gleams like this no other time—
the slick oil bringing forth the wood.

We all become fat—the pot, the fire,
the lard jars that I ladle into,
the dirt. The black kettle cools.

Lush beads slide down the metal bevel,
condense in the clumped cracklings
at the bottom. I spear one crisp

and tender bit of rendered fat,
heedless of the grease I smear
on tongue and lips and cheeks.

I will wash with warm and soapy
water, but I, paddle, pot, or ground,
will never forget this fatness.

Eating My Heart

. . . they would have swallowed us up alive,
when their anger was kindled against us . . .
Psalm 124:3, RSV

You don't know, Preacher, how hard it is
        to come to God. If God is Father.
                If you speak to me of a father's love.

Every day he told me he loved me, then
        he cut me up. It was as if
                I were Olaudah Equiano

on the slave ship. Dad would give me
        a quadrant, show me the stars,
                then slap me back in chains.

I didn't know his tongue; his speech
        was English to my African ears,
                and his great copper pot could be

for my flesh. I was Crusoe on the shores
        of Tobago, finding the scattered
                charred bones the cannibals

had left behind. I did not know when
        he would slip his canoe from the mainland,
                sail across the Orinoco

to my lost island and eat me alive.
        I was the poor of Ireland, and he
                a Swift suggesting smugly

the solution to my impoverished
        state, my baby ways. Sell me on
                the meat market. I was tender

enough for boiling or frying, a fricassee
     or a ragout. The callous indifferent
          world would be fatter for the sale,

and he, the seller, would be fatter too.
     How many times has he, lovingly,
          put his arm around my shoulders,

pulled me off the street, like Jeffrey Dahmer
     whispering words of love to me.
          I could never read motive

in that handsome face. I was dazed before
     he drugged me, eaten before he cut out
          my heart to have it for dinner.

Safe Houses

For the enemy has pursued me;
he has crushed my life to the ground;
he has made me sit in darkness like those long dead.
Psalm 143:3, RSV

The angel asks,
Why do you seek the living among the dead?

Compassion International
advertises how I can feed, help educate, perhaps save
one child for $32 a month.
I Google the website,
read testimonials, see pinched faces,
eyes like forgotten pennies,
brown and lustrous as mud puddles.
I get lost in the report
heard quickly on a radio ad,
how orphans seek refuge in a graveyard,
the safest place they've found.

I go on to my father's story:
Before Phillipsbourg, France,
the night falling in on them,
soldiers dig trenches—scraping and gouging,
deeper deeper, overhead
mortars whistle,
earth rucks upward, showers them in dirt.
They dig, madly
before headstones, listening.
They have learned the signature—
the eerie whine of a shell that beds too close.
Mausoleums cast shadows
in the half-light of bombs,
prefiguring them with darkness.
Praying for blessings in the black earth,
praying for safety among the dead
among boon companions
they dig.

The dead may haunt
but the living kill.
Where is safety
when the dead are the last retreat?

God and War: the Sacred and the Scared

And by my God I can leap over a wall.
        Psalm 18:29, RSV

You volunteered and lied about your age,
        fresh from early graduation,
        curly-haired, sandy-eyed, slight of build.
Wiry, you could climb a rope,
        feet dangling, hand over hand,
        or lope across plowed land, not stumbling.
You took the eye God gave you,
        marksman in the hunt for squirrels,
        you took the heart that beat within you.

And now you've leaped this wall
        somewhere in France; war-ripped,
        explosives whining, rubble falling.
Bright as piedmont fields, despite the smoke,
        a shaft of sunlight on this southern side,
        you cradle rations, a beaten can.
The gold of peaches like the gold of sun
        shines as jewels before you,
        beats like longing for the fields of home.

What a long leap you have made,
        across the many waters,
        into the face of tyranny and hate!
What justice you've upheld, allegiance,
        the stars of heaven and the flag,
        the red stripes of former battlefields.
Red stripes, red scars, red bombs bursting,
        a long leap from pastoral fields:
        Patriotism, peaches, at the front.

The Organization of Mourning:
An Open Letter to My Wife

When the cares of my heart are many,
        thy consolations cheer my soul.
                Psalm 94:19, RSV

You played with the flowers, a daisy petal,
fragment of carnation, scrap of rose left behind
in the funeral home's van your father drove, parked
soberly in your drive. Your obsequies over
insect tombs with your cousin were mock serious,
the grave foreshadowings of ancient death.
How brave the flower bits showed
for a time. So my grandmother played
in her grandfather's coffin, he in his nineties,
readying. Hide and seek. Or a clever place
to take a nap. She was a bit of flower
dimming in his eyes.

                You and I.
We have been taught and teach of death,
I stand at the head, over and over,
and you appear among the mourners,
the neon Astroturf carpet laid upon
sere drought of summer, snow of winter.
The graveyard is cold or hot, windy or wet.
Tent edges flap, the sun casts shadows.
Sprays lean to look in at the grave
on a hillside plot, unsteady ground.
We each do our part to raise resurrection,
to remind a folk we love of the folk they love,
that the dead do not stay dead.

                When you die
I must not grieve beyond a limit.
I will find, I think, a gathering of daisies,
a little color, bright though brief,
and pull each petal, tug by tug,

say God loves me God loves me
God loves me He loves me
until consolation comes,
rises like a heap of petals
about my feet.

Best Intentions

For not from the east or from the west
and not from the wilderness comes lifting up . .. .
Psalm 75:6, RSV

So I gave you the stove. It took a wrecking
    ball almost to unsettle the old one
        so tightly snugged in the baseboard counter.

After ten years of marriage, I could think
    it had grown there. You halted me, unbalanced
        as I was, to dump the drawers in a headlong rattle.

I eased the lumbersome thing through the constraining
    doorframe of the kitchen, built nonstandard, off-plumb
        like everything else in our century-old farm house.

You had often fussed about the old stove's eyes,
    how they lost their heat, how you had to shake up
        a pot to reestablish a connection, keep things hot.

I took your complaints for dissatisfaction,
    thought the surprise would please you, as I mean
        to please you. You crumpled with your cookbooks

in the floor like wreckage, crying over the change.
    There was no drawer to hold your tested and untested
        recipes, no assurance that the gleaming new surface

would stand abuse, no guarantee a cake would rise.
    You were the one down on the floor, fingering the black
        tire mark of the handtruck, but I was down there with you.

Table Syrup, Cigarettes, and the Blind

Teach me thy way, O Lord,
that I may walk in thy truth ...
Psalm 86:11, RSV

When I decided to burn
candles one winter
(calling poems out of
bayberry, wintergreen,
one more magical
prestidigitation)
I wanted an ashtray
for struck matches.

The only one we thought of
was Coke-bottle green,
a second grade gift
my wife had made her parents,
the picture of her face
looking up through glass.
I couldn't snub matches
against such hopeful eyes.

My father smokes a pipe
so I asked my parents.
My mother brought me
dried out terrapin shells,
some with outer armor
chipped, neat rectangles
missing. I took to my study
one brown bit of earth child.

I became, as a result,
more aware of ashtrays,
relics of Americana,
tobacco stub palaces.
My mother-in-law's home
honors my wife's baby shoes,

coated now in bronze,
feet stilled before an ashtray.

But oddest bowl of all
the blue green ceramic
my aunt gave me. I begged
it from her when I was small
because I liked King's syrup
swirled with homemade butter.
The alphabet circles
the bowl's flat edge.

How many biscuits
I sopped beneath the raised dots
of the Braille alphabet,
not knowing the bowl's white cane
was not a candy cane,
not knowing the rim's indentations
were for cigarettes,
not knowing the ways of my time.

The Ground from Which He Was Taken

. . . venom like the venom of a serpent . . .
Psalm 58:4, RSV

I have seen
colors of warning
fluorescent orange, schoolbus yellow,
optic apple green
even from the corners
of my eyes

in a pile of locust posts
a crevice of a sow's stall
along a fence line
in the chicken house shadows
under the step just taken
coiled in the delivered mail
slipping from under the piano
I have seen the deadliest colors
the quickest glimpse
full warning

cat-slit topaz eyes
orange, like dead leaves
dull but screaming orange

I fear most
pulling back a tomato vine
to see them
waiting
on the cool ground
beneath sustaining fruit

dusk orange diamonds
deepening the garden ground
waiting
that god-awful thickness
flat head and s-curve

stupefying fear
and one more warning
of limitless God

Snake Canes for Sale

. . . those who hate thee have
raised their heads. They lay crafty
plans against thy people . . .
Psalm 83:2-3, RSV

friends bring the craftsman
tree and vine, stock to whittle
a woodburnt stubble

of crosshatch coils up
under his tools, slits appear
eyes unblinking wink

each Virginia snake
writhes to new incarnation
tempting me to buy

but hand on canehead
snake's tongue a finger away
surely I'll stumble

Greening

. . . they flourish in the courts of our God.
They still bring forth fruit in old age,
they are ever full of sap and green . . .
Psalm 92:14, RSV

The triangular tip of the high carbon knife,
dull gray to rust color down the backbone of its length,
this kitchen knife kept sharp by the grit
of the worn-away whetstone—the tip placed just so,
slid under the green whorl of leaves
that look like a green petticoat or flounce
ruffling from under an outer dress,
the tip under the whorl to snip the white tap root.

Then the airy crest of creasy seems to float—
but really the fall is slight—
into the brown grocery bag that I carry—
the brown filling bag that becomes
ever more airy. One crown-like crest of creasy
after another, one tumbling somersault of smell
of iron to mingle with other greening smells.
We press down but outward they spring.

I see also my mother dressed in Sunday best,
not the work clothes—including pants—
she most often wears. Somehow, she is dressed again
in gray silk with pleats and gathers, tucked at the waist
and flowing and billowing in a free cascade
of spring air, as if she held onto a Maypole
and whirled about. I can see her smile
and pull my head into the silk and ruffle my hair.

The gathering of greens mingles and mixes
with the settled air of Sunday mornings.
I lay on the hard bench of sermons
yet to be understood. Perhaps I understood,
though dimly, the placement of my head

on that lap of silk. I understand better now.
Holding my child's hand, I take a bag for greens,
and we go out to feed the present or the future.

ABOUT THE POET

Charles A. Swanson grew up on a farm, and still lives with his wife
on what his family would call a "postage stamp" farm at the foot of
Turkeycock Mountain in Pittsylvania County, Virginia,
not far from the home of his paternal ancestors.
He has a love for the things of the earth, and he believes in
both a sustainable agriculture and a sustainable faith.
His poems and short fiction have appeared in journals and
publications throughout the Appalachian region.

Teacher of the Year at Gretna High School in 2007-2008,
he instructs students in Creative Writing,
dual enrollment English and AP English.
He won the James Still Award for Poetry (2005),
among other honors, and a chapbook of his
poems, *Farm Life and Legend*, is due for release
by Finishing Line Press in the fall of 2009.
He pastors Melville Avenue Baptist Church
in Danville, Virginia.

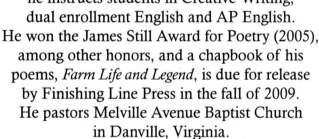

Breinigsville, PA USA
21 March 2011
258108BV00001B/44/P